GEMSTONES OF THE WORLD

RUMMAGING FOR RUBIES

HEATHER MOORE NIVER

PowerKiDS
press™
New York

Published in 2018 by The Rosen Publishing Group, Inc.
29 East 21st Street, New York, NY 10010

First Edition

Editor: Theresa Morlock
Book Design: Reann Nye

Photo Credits: Cover NIK/Shutterstock.com; p. 4 Gems Collection/Shutterstock.com; p. 5 Tarzhanova/Shutterstock.com; p. 6 Imfoto/Shutterstock.com; p. 7 boykung/Shutterstock.com; p. 8 De Agostini Picture Library/De Agostini/Getty Images; p. 9 Perfectgemstore/Shutterstock.com; pp. 10, 17 Yut chanthaburi/Shutterstock.com; p. 11 Yves GELLIE/Gamma-Rapho/Getty Images; p. 12 Nika Lerman/Shutterstock.com; p. 13 DEA / A.RIZZI/De Agostini/Getty Images; p. 14 S_E/Shutterstock.com; p. 15 Potapov Alexander/Shutterstock.com; p. 16 STUDIO492/Shutterstock.com; p. 18 Michael Freeman/Corbis Documentary/Getty Images; p. 19 Bloomberg/Getty Images; p. 20 EM Karuna/Shutterstock.com; p. 21 Science & Society Picture Library/SSPL/Getty Images; p. 22 Pisut Phaetrangsee/Shutterstock.com.

Cataloging-in-Publication Data

Names: Niver, Heather Moore.
Title: Rummaging for rubies / Heather Moore Niver.
Description: New York : PowerKids Press, 2018. | Series: Gemstones of the world | Includes index.
Identifiers: ISBN 9781538328293 (pbk.) | ISBN 9781508164203 (library bound) | ISBN 9781538328354 (6 pack)
Subjects: LCSH: Rubies–Juvenile literature. | Mineralogy–Juvenile literature.
Classification: LCC QE394.R8 N56 2018 | DDC 553.8'4–dc23

Manufactured in the United States of America

CPSIA Compliance Information: Batch Batch #BW18PK: For Further Information contact Rosen Publishing, New York, New York at 1-800-237-9932

CONTENTS

RARE RUBIES

A bright red ruby will always catch your eye. This brilliant gemstone is very **rare** and difficult to find. Large, clear rubies are even more rare than diamonds. One good ruby might be worth millions of dollars. Rubies are tough, too. Diamonds are one of the very few gemstones harder than rubies.

How exactly do these magnificent gems form? What do people use them for? Ready to learn more about this strong and splendid gem? Let's go **rummage** up some rubies!

HIDDEN GEMS

People have been using rubies for a long time. Like many other gemstones, they were once thought to have magic or power. In Burma, warriors put rubies beneath their skin! They believed these powerful stones would protect them from harm.

Rubies are the July birthstone.

RECOGNIZING A RUBY

All gemstones are organized by basic physical properties, or features. You can recognize a ruby by identifying these features.

- The **luster** of polished ruby is quite bright. Before they are polished, rubies look dull and waxy.

- A stone's hardness tells you how likely it is that something will scratch its surface. Rubies are very hard.

- Some rubies are transparent, or clear, but others are opaque, or cloudy.

- Of course, rubies are shades of red. The most valuable rubies are a bright red.

HIDDEN GEMS

The hardness of a gemstone is measured on a scale of 1 to 10 called the Mohs' scale. Talc is the softest **mineral**. Diamonds are the hardest at 10, and rubies are a 9.

Rubies can be purple to almost pink. Color is the most important property when it comes to the gemstone's value.

COLOR CODE

Rubies and sapphires are both forms of corundum. Corundum is a naturally colorless mineral. Different colors occur when other **materials** are present. Only the red stones are rubies. Sapphires are usually blue corundum. But any color corundum besides red is considered sapphire. Sapphires that aren't blue are called fancy sapphires or given a special color name.

If a ruby contains other minerals, it may also have a special way of **reflecting** light. When polished, some stones reflect light in a star shape.

HIDDEN GEMS

Heating rubies can remove cloudy areas, but heated rubies are not quite as valuable as those that are bright and clear naturally. When heated, rubies turn bright green! They return to red when they cool.

Pigeon-blood red is the darkest, and most valuable, shade of ruby. An element called chromium gives the ruby its red color.

WHERE IN THE WORLD ARE RUBIES?

Rubies are found in a number of countries. Many rubies are found in Myanmar, Thailand, Sri Lanka, and Tanzania. People sometimes find rubies in India and Pakistan, as well as Madagascar, Zimbabwe, Afghanistan, Kenya, and Cambodia. Rubies and sapphires are also found in the United States in North Carolina and elsewhere.

The largest ruby certified by the Gemology Institute of America is the 125West ruby. It weighs 8.2 pounds (3.7 kg), which is 18,696 **carats**. Nobody knows where it came from!

HIDDEN GEMS

For many years, the Rajaratna ruby, which weighs 2,475 carats, was considered the largest in the world. Then the 125West ruby was discovered.

Myanmar is the world's largest producer of rubies.

RUBIES IN THE RAW

Rubies are a kind of crystal. One way that crystals form is when a liquid becomes a solid. Think of water turning into ice. As it freezes, the **molecules** line up and fuse, or join, in a pattern. This process is called crystallization. Hot liquid or soft rock called magma can crystallize too. If it cools slowly, crystals such as rubies, emeralds, and diamonds may form.

Rubies can also be made in a laboratory. At first, scientists fused small pieces of natural ruby together to make bigger rubies.

Rubies are formed when hot, liquid magma cools into a solid. They can take millions of years to form.

MAKING RUBIES

Synthetic, or artificial, rubies can be made from other materials in several different ways. One of the most popular is a process called flame fusion. Powdered gem ingredients are heated until they melt. Then they're cooled so crystals form.

People may make fake rubies, diamonds, and emeralds out of glass called "paste." Paste gems are not as bright or hard as real gemstones made naturally. Synthetic rubies are more affordable than rubies that were formed naturally.

GARNET

HIDDEN GEMS

Natural red rubies are sometimes called oriental rubies. This is to set them apart from other stones. For example, Cape rubies, Australian rubies, and Arizona rubies are actually garnets, another kind of red stone.

Not all rubies come from nature.
People make some in laboratories.
Only stones that are found in nature
can be called gemstones.

15

DIGGING 'EM UP!

Some rubies are dug out of the earth. The rock must be chipped away from the rubies. Another method is the sluice method, which involves washing soil away in a long container called a trough, which has small holes in the bottom. People examine the remaining rock and soil by hand.

Rubies may be polished for a smooth look. Or they may be cut to have many sparkling sides. Cut and polished rubies can then be made into **jewelry**.

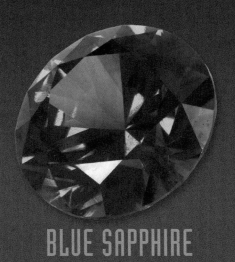

BLUE SAPPHIRE

HIDDEN GEMS

Sometimes rubies and sapphires are freed from the ground by erosion, which means the wearing away of Earth's surface by wind or water. Then they may wash into nearby streams. The stones can be found in the gravel of these streams.

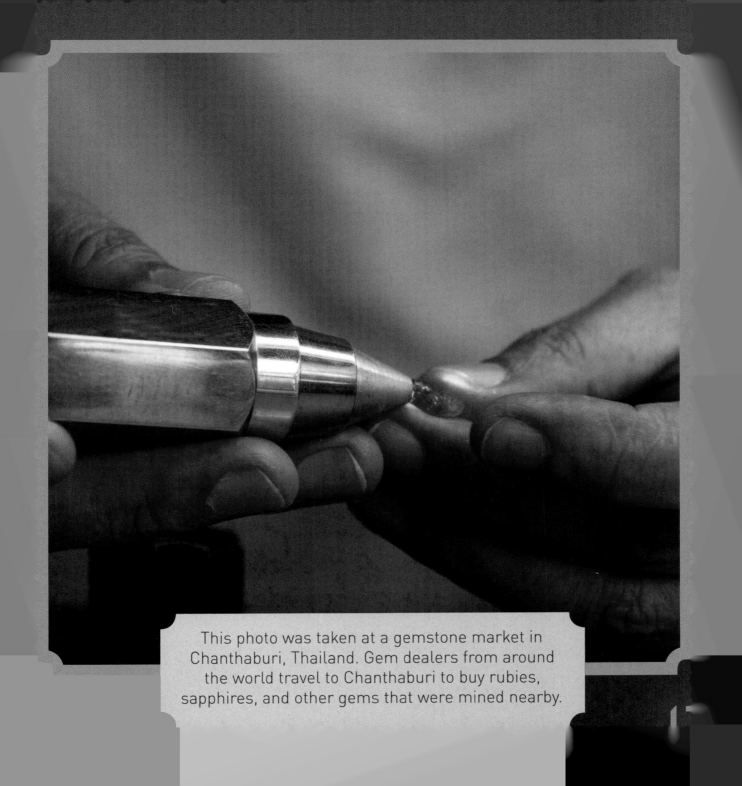

This photo was taken at a gemstone market in Chanthaburi, Thailand. Gem dealers from around the world travel to Chanthaburi to buy rubies, sapphires, and other gems that were mined nearby.

EFFECTS OF MINING

Mining rubies takes a lot of time and money. It's difficult to mine rubies without breaking or cracking them. Also, the digging process may harm the **environment**.

When people find a new source for rubies (or other gems), there might be a "gem rush." Hundreds of eager gem hunters come to the area. They dig big pits in the ground that may never be filled back in. Mining can lead to deforestation. This is when trees are cleared from an area.

The huge pits required for mining rubies or other gemstones are just one example of the effect the process can have on the environment.

A USEFUL GEM

Historically, rubies were made into beautiful jewelry worn by the wealthy and powerful. Some of the most famous rubies belonged to queens who wore them on crowns and necklaces. Rubies are more than just beautiful gemstones, though. Besides sparkling on jewelry such as necklaces, rings, and bracelets, rubies play an important part in science.

Theodore Maiman made the first ruby **laser** in 1960. It used man-made ruby crystals. Today, most lasers are made from other materials because they're more affordable.

HIDDEN GEMS

Rubies and other man-made stones are used in wristwatches. They help the watch keep time. Rubies and other hard stones are useful because they can be polished smooth and do not wear out much over time.

Ruby lasers are used for making **holograms**. They're also used for heavy-duty cutting and **welding**.

21

History shows records of rubies that date as far back as AD 600. Warriors believed the red gemstones gave them protection during battles. More recently, in *The Wizard of Oz* movie, Dorothy's ruby slippers helped her get home.

Far below Earth's surface, magma cools very slowly to make rubies. It takes millions of years for a ruby to form naturally. Natural rubies are quite rare. They are strong and beautiful, a combination that might give the ruby its sense of magic.

GLOSSARY

carat: The unit of weight by which gemstones are measured.

environment: The natural world around us.

hologram: A three-dimensional image formed by light beams.

jewelry: Objects people wear on their body for decoration, often made of special metals or prized stones.

laser: A device that produces a narrow beam of light.

luster: The sheen or glow of a reflective surface.

material: Something from which something else can be made.

mineral: A naturally occurring solid substance that is not of plant or animal origin.

molecule: The smallest possible amount of something that has all the characteristics of that thing.

rare: Uncommon and special.

reflect: To throw back light, heat, or sound without absorbing it, or taking it in.

rummage: To search for something.

weld: To join two pieces of metal together by melting them.

INDEX

WEBSITES

Due to the changing nature of Internet links, PowerKids Press has developed an online list of websites related to the subject of this book. This site is updated regularly. Please use this link to access the list: www.powerkidslinks.com/gotw/ruby